WITHDRAWN

A Crabtree Branches Book

Today's Stars

LADY GAGA

Samantha Bell

Crabtree Publishing
crabtreebooks.com

School-to-Home Support for Caregivers and Teachers

This high-interest book is designed to motivate striving students with engaging topics while building fluency, vocabulary, and an interest in reading. Here are a few questions and activities to help the reader build upon his or her comprehension skills.

Before Reading:
- *What do I think this book is about?*
- *What do I know about this topic?*
- *What do I want to learn about this topic?*
- *Why am I reading this book?*

During Reading:
- *I wonder why...*
- *I'm curious to know...*
- *How is this like something I already know?*
- *What have I learned so far?*

After Reading:
- *What was the author trying to teach me?*
- *What are some details?*
- *How did the photographs and captions help me understand more?*
- *Read the book again and look for the vocabulary words.*
- *What questions do I still have?*

Extension Activities:
- *What was your favorite part of the book? Write a paragraph on it.*
- *Draw a picture of your favorite thing you learned from the book.*

TABLE OF CONTENTS

Always Something New	4
Safety in Music	8
Rise to Stardom	12
A Music Sensation	16
On the Big Screen	20
Making Kindness Cool Again	24
Glossary	30
Index	31
Websites to Visit	31
About the Author	32

ALWAYS SOMETHING NEW

Lady Gaga is a songwriter and pop star. She is known for her unique styles of music. Her songs often sound like a cross between pop, dance, and electronic. But Lady Gaga is also a serious actress.

In the first part of her career, she was known for her **eccentric** fashion choices. Today, she is known for receiving major awards. This ability to change her image has kept her on top.

Fun Facts

Lady Gaga often displays an unusual sense of style. One dress she wore looked like a giant silver **sea urchin** with blow-up spines.

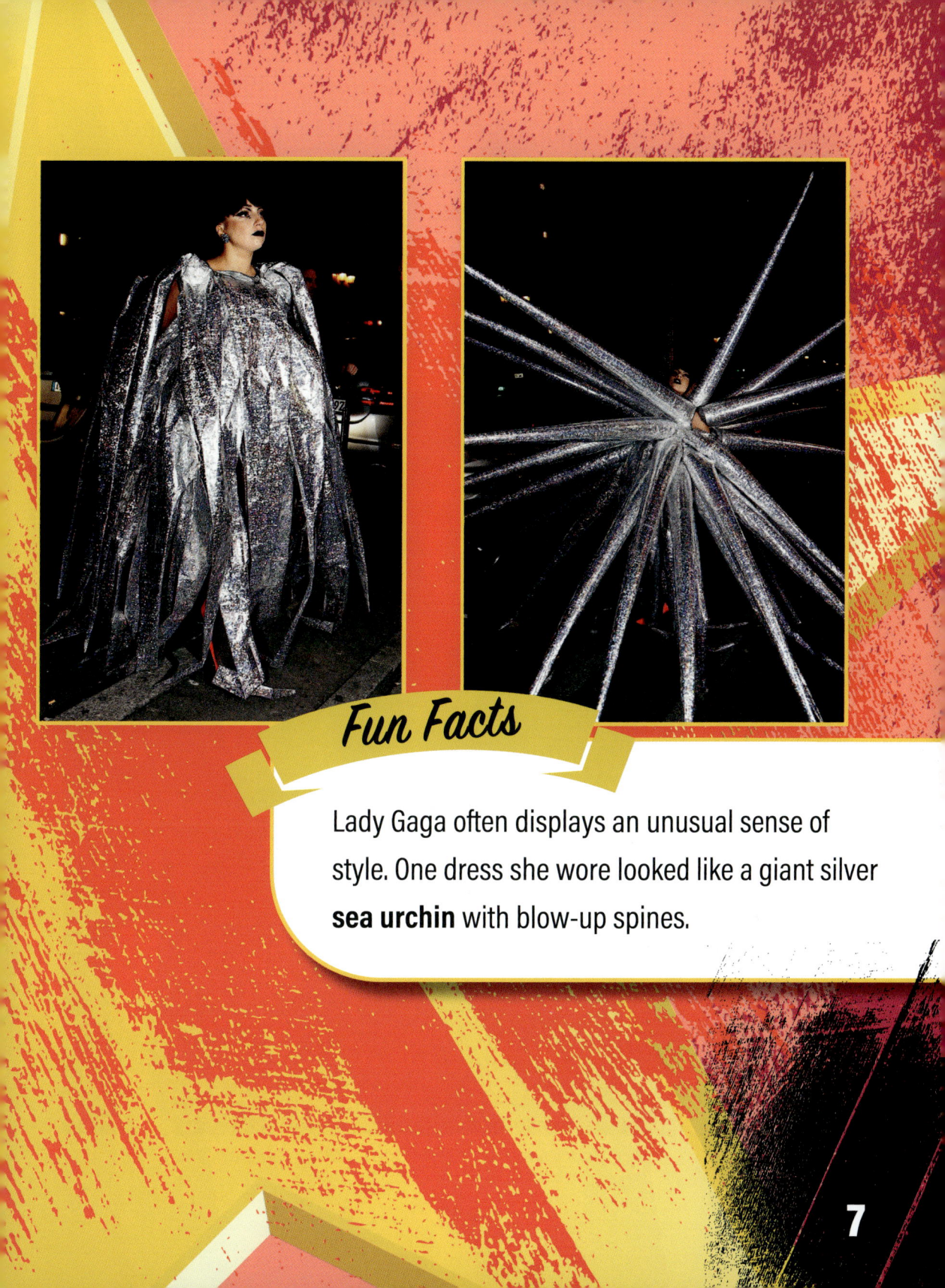

SAFETY IN MUSIC

Lady Gaga was born on March 28, 1986, to Cynthia and Joseph Germanotta. They named her Stefani Joanne Angelina. They lived in New York City, where Stefani and her younger sister Natali attended a private school. But Stefani was often bullied at school. She felt **anxious**, insecure, and depressed.

Lady Gaga's parents, Joseph and Cynthia Germanotta

Lady Gaga

Music became very important to Stefani. She took singing lessons and performed in school **musicals**. When Stefani was 17, she was accepted to New York University's art school. While there, she worked on her songwriting skills. When she was 19, she left to pursue a music career.

Lady Gaga as a student at Convent of the Sacred Heart, a private all-girls' school in New York City

Fun Facts

Stefani began playing the piano when she was four years old. She learned to **play by ear**.

RISE TO STARDOM

After she left school, Stefani wrote songs for other singers, including Britney Spears and New Kids on the Block.

Britney Spears

New Kids on the Block

In 2006, she met music **producer** Rob Fusari. They began writing songs together, adding dance beats to the music.

Lady Gaga and Rob Fusari

During this time, Rob began calling Stefani "Gaga" when she came into the studio. The name came from a 1984 song by the rock band Queen called "Radio Ga Ga." Stefani liked the name and wanted to **reinvent** herself as a performer. In 2007, she signed her first record deal as Lady Gaga.

"Just Dance" was released on April 8, 2008, as the lead single from Lady Gaga's debut studio album, The Fame.

Fun Facts

Lady Gaga wrote the song "Just Dance" with producer RedOne in only about 10 minutes.

A MUSIC SENSATION

In 2008, Lady Gaga released her first album, called *The Fame*. She was 22 years old. The album included the hits "Just Dance" and "Poker Face." Almost overnight, Lady Gaga became a success.

In 2009, Lady Gaga went on tour in Europe as an opening act for the group The Pussycat Dolls. Then she did her own tour in the United States called "The Fame Ball Tour." Since then, her music hits and awards keep coming.

Lady Gaga at the launch party for her perfume Fame in 2012

Fun Facts

In 2012, Lady Gaga created a new perfume called Fame. It appears black in the bottle. But when it is sprayed, the liquid is clear.

ON THE BIG SCREEN

Lady Gaga wanted to be an actress more than a singer, but at first she was bad at **auditioning**. In 2013, she began getting movie roles. One of her biggest roles was in the 2018 film *A Star Is Born*.

Bradley Cooper and Lady Gaga in the 2018 film A Star Is Born.

Lady Gaga plays Harley Quinn in the upcoming movie Joker: Folie à Deux.

Fun Facts

Lady Gaga's first onscreen acting role was in 2001. She played a teen girl in a swimming pool scene.

Lady Gaga was **nominated** for an Academy Award, or Oscar, for her role in *A Star Is Born*. Although she did not win that award, she did win an Oscar for the movie's song "Shallow."

In 2019, she became the first woman to win an Oscar, a Grammy Award, a British Academy of Film Award, and a Golden Globe Award in one single year.

MAKING KINDNESS COOL AGAIN

Because she was bullied as a teenager, Lady Gaga wants to encourage people to be brave and kind.

Fun Facts

In November 2018, the SAG-AFTRA Foundation presented Lady Gaga with their Artists Inspiration Award. The award honors artists who use their fame to help others.

25

In 2012, Lady Gaga and her mother started a **nonprofit** organization called Born This Way Foundation. Its goal is to support the mental health of young people and work with them to build a kinder world.

Lady Gaga and her mom Cynthia Germanotta

Lady Gaga wants young people to feel like their emotions are understood and accepted. She also wants to change the way people view mental health issues.

Lady Gaga is showing the world all she has to offer as she continues to reinvent herself. Whether a pop star or a movie star, she **strives** to be true to herself.

GLOSSARY

anxious (ANG-shuhs): Feeling worried or nervous about something that might happen

audition (aw-DISH-uhn): To try out for a part in a movie, TV show, or play

eccentric (ek-SEN-trik): Unusual

musical (MYOO-zi-kuhl): A play or movie that tells a story with songs and dancing

nominate (NAH-mi-nayt): To choose someone as a candidate for an award

nonprofit (non-PROF-it): An organization that uses the money it earns to help people or support something

play by ear (PLAY BAI EER): To play music by hearing it, without needing to read it

producer (pruh-DOO-ser): A person who oversees the making of a music recording

reinvent (ree-in-VENT): To become a different kind of person or performer

sea urchin (SEE UR-chin): A small sea animal that is covered in sharp spines

strive (STRYV): To work very hard to do something

INDEX

awards 6, 18, 22, 23, 25

childhood 8, 10, 11

family 8, 26

fashion 6, 7

mental health 8, 24, 26, 28

movies 20, 21, 22, 23

music 4, 10, 11, 12, 13, 14, 15, 16, 18, 22

nonprofit 26, 28

school 8, 10

songwriting 10, 12, 13, 15

WEBSITES TO VISIT

https://bornthisway.foundation/

www.biography.com/musician/lady-gaga

https://kids.britannica.com/students/article/Lady-Gaga/544331

ABOUT THE AUTHOR

Samantha Bell lives with her family in the foothills of the Blue Ridge Mountains. She has four gray cats with a lot of attitude. When she's not writing, she likes to draw, hike, and visit new places.

Written by: Samantha Bell
Designed by: Kathy Walsh
Series Development: James Earley
Proofreader: Melissa Boyce
Educational Consultant: Marie Lemke M.Ed.

Photographs: Shutterstock, Newscom: Cover, Title pg, Backgrounds: Cat Morley / Avalon@Newscom, Anna Davidovskaya, StockAppeal, Vector Tradition, Miloje; p 5, 17: StockAppeal; p 7, 11, 14, 19, 21, 25: Vector Tradition; p 3: Nicola Marfisi/Avalon; p 4: Ian West; p 5: DFree; p 6: KCS Presse/Splash News; p 6: KCS Presse/Splash News, Marco Iacobucci Epp, Matteo Chinellato; p 7: KCS Presse/Splash News; p 8: Terrence Jennings; p 9, 10, 11: Splash News; P 12: Photo By Adam Scull/PHOTOlink.net, Tom Donoghue; p 13: Agencia El Universal p 14: Agencia el Universal; p 15: Roger Williams; p 16: Christine Chew; p 17: DMS/HS1; p 18: Splash News; p 19 Kristin Callahan/Everett Collection, @ Wiki; p 20: Gerber Pictures; p 21: BeautifulSignatureIG/SplashNews; p 22: Lumeimages; p 23: Alberto Rodriguez, Armando Arorizo; p 24: Violetta Markelou/Splash News; p 25: Joe Sutter/PacificCoastNews; p 26: Sonia Moskowitz; p 27: B4859/Avalon; p 28: Splash News; p 29: Ferrari; p 31: Jim Ruymen

Crabtree Publishing

crabtreebooks.com   800-387-7650

Copyright © 2025 Crabtree Publishing

All rights reserved. No part of this publication may be reproduced, stored in a retrieval system or be transmitted in any form or by any means, electronic, mechanical, photocopying, recording, or otherwise, without the prior written permission of Crabtree Publishing.

Printed in the USA/062024/CG20240201

Published in Canada
Crabtree Publishing
616 Welland Ave.
St. Catharines, Ontario
L2M 5V6

Published in the United States
Crabtree Publishing
347 Fifth Ave
Suite 1402-145
New York, NY 10016

Library and Archives Canada Cataloguing in Publication
Available at Library and Archives Canada

Library of Congress Cataloging-in-Publication Data
Available at the Library of Congress

Hardcover: 978-1-0398-3910-6
Paperback: 978-1-0398-3995-3
Ebook (pdf): 978-1-0398-4067-6
Epub: 978-1-0398-4139-0